WORLD STUDIES

CENTRAL AMERICA

by Emma Huddleston

FOCUS
READERS®

V☉YAGER

www.focusreaders.com

Focus Readers is distributed by North Star Editions:
sales@northstareditions.com | 888-417-0195

Produced for Focus Readers by Red Line Editorial.

Content Consultant: Jennifer Carolina Gómez Menjívar, PhD, Associate Professor of World Languages and Cultures, University of Minnesota Duluth

Photographs ©: Shutterstock Images, cover, 1, 4–5, 7, 8–9, 11, 15, 16–17, 19, 20–21, 22, 25, 31, 45; P. W. Hamilton/AP Images, 13; iStockphoto, 27; Camilo Freedman/Zuma Press/Newscom, 28–29; Red Line Editorial, 33; John Stillwell/PA Wire URN:16918851/AP Images, 34–35; Jorge Cabera/Reuters/Newscom, 37; Alfredo Zuniga/AP Images, 39; Nano Calvo/VWPics/AP Images, 40–41; Carlo Bevilacqua/SIPA/Newscom, 43

Library of Congress Cataloging-in-Publication Data
Names: Huddleston, Emma, author.
Title: Central America / by Emma Huddleston.
Description: Lake Elmo, MN : Focus Readers, [2021] | Series: World studies |
    Includes index. | Audience: Grades 7-9
Identifiers: LCCN 2019057437 (print) | LCCN 2019057438 (ebook) | ISBN
    9781644933985 (hardcover) | ISBN 9781644934746 (paperback) | ISBN
    9781644936269 (pdf) | ISBN 9781644935507 (ebook)
Subjects: LCSH: Central America--Juvenile literature.
Classification: LCC F1428.5 .H83 2021 (print) | LCC F1428.5 (ebook) | DDC
    972.8--dc23
LC record available at https://lccn.loc.gov/2019057437
LC ebook record available at https://lccn.loc.gov/2019057438

Printed in the United States of America
Mankato, MN
012021

ABOUT THE AUTHOR

Emma Huddleston lives in the Twin Cities with her husband. She enjoys reading, writing, and swing dancing. When she visited Costa Rica, she was amazed by the beautiful land and wildlife.

TABLE OF CONTENTS

CHAPTER I
Welcome to Central America 5

CHAPTER 2
History of Central America 9

CULTURE PROFILE
Maya Peoples 14

CHAPTER 3
Geography and Climate 17

CHAPTER 4
Plants and Animals 21

ANIMAL PROFILE
Birds of Central America 26

CHAPTER 5
Natural Resources and Economy 29

CHAPTER 6
Government and Politics 35

CHAPTER 7
People and Culture 41

Focus on Central America • 46
Glossary • 47
To Learn More • 48
Index • 48

CHAPTER 1

WELCOME TO CENTRAL AMERICA

A thin body of land connects North America and South America. Rainforests and mountains surround the region's towns and cities. This area is known as Central America. It is home to an incredible amount of diversity.

Seven countries make up Central America. Belize and Guatemala are the most northern countries in the region. These countries share a border with the North American nation of Mexico.

Five of the seven Central American countries have coasts along both the Caribbean Sea and the Pacific Ocean.

El Salvador, Honduras, Nicaragua, and Costa Rica are in the middle of Central America. Panama is the region's most southern country. It borders the South American nation of Colombia.

Some cities and towns in Central America are full of history. For instance, Joya de Cerén is an ancient village in El Salvador. It was frozen in time by a volcanic eruption. Other cities are full of people and businesses. Panama City, Panama, is a modern urban center. It has skyscrapers and shops. The city is also home to the Panama Canal, an important shipping point. Ships from many countries travel through this canal. Factories in Tegucigalpa, Honduras, fuel that country's economy. The city's factories produce a variety of products, including plastics and tires.

More than 2.5 million people live in Guatemala City, Guatemala. It is the largest city in Central

America. Its cultural history dates back to the 1700s. Today, the city features several museums and government buildings.

Beyond the cities lie a variety of rural landscapes. Central America is home to rainforests, mountains, and more.

CENTRAL AMERICA

GUATEMALA
BELIZE
HONDURAS
EL SALVADOR
NICARAGUA
COSTA RICA
PANAMA
CARIBBEAN SEA
PACIFIC OCEAN

N
W E
S

CHAPTER 2

HISTORY OF CENTRAL AMERICA

Humans have lived in Central America for at least 10,000 years. Early people hunted and gathered for food. They did not live in one place for very long. But over thousands of years, people began growing crops. They mainly farmed squash, corn, and beans. Groups of people settled in certain areas and formed villages.

In the 1800s BCE, the Barra culture developed. These people lived in present-day Guatemala.

Corn was the most important crop for many early Central American peoples.

They also lived in El Salvador. The Barra made some of the first clay pottery in Central America.

Societies in Central America continued to become more complex. In the 1500s BCE, the Maya **civilization** began. The Maya were not one single culture. Instead, the civilization included several people groups, such as the K'iche' and Mopan. Between 250 and 900 CE, the Maya were their most powerful. They lived in more than 40 cities across the region.

Maya civilization declined in the 900s. But smaller groups continued to develop. For example, the Pipil left Mexico in the 1000s. They traveled south through Guatemala and El Salvador. Some stayed there. Others pushed farther south into Nicaragua. By 1500, millions of people lived in Central America. Groups made art, traded with one another, and sometimes fought.

△ Many ancient Maya buildings survive today, including the Xunantunich ceremonial center in Belize.

However, Central America changed quickly in the 1500s. Spanish **conquistadores** invaded. They took over much of the region. This invasion devastated Central America's **Indigenous** peoples. The Spanish killed and enslaved large numbers of people. The Spanish also brought diseases with them. Indigenous people were not used to those diseases. As a result, millions of people died.

Even so, Indigenous peoples resisted Spanish rule. The Miskito kingdom in Nicaragua became allies with England. And the Itzá in Guatemala kept their independence until 1697.

Spain's control over Central America weakened in the 1700s. By 1840, most Central American countries had become independent. Panama, however, was part of Colombia. And in 1862, Belize became a British colony.

Panama did not become independent until 1903. But that same year, the United States bought the rights to the Panama Canal. The canal was completed in 1914. The United States controlled other parts of the region, too. By 1909, the United States had helped overthrow Nicaragua's leader. Then it built military bases in the country. And by the 1910s, a US company controlled most of Honduras's banana industry.

▲ Guatemala's civil war lasted 36 years, from 1960 to 1996.

In the mid-1900s, Central America experienced another huge shift. Several military governments came to power. In response, civil wars broke out in Costa Rica, Guatemala, El Salvador, and Nicaragua. The United States involved itself in all of these wars. It also invaded Panama in 1989.

The region's most recent peace treaty was signed in 1996. But the history of this important region affects its nations and peoples to this day.

MAYA PEOPLES

The Maya are Indigenous peoples of Central America and Mexico. They have been living in the region for thousands of years. Early Maya developed great skills in math, astronomy, and architecture. Their achievements were advanced for the time. For example, they built irrigation systems. These systems directed water throughout their cities and land. Early Maya also built stone temples and pyramids. They built these structures without wheels or metal tools.

In addition, the Maya developed one of the world's earliest systems of math. They created a calendar as well. It had 365 days per year, which is the same as most calendars today. The Maya used a written language, too. And they created modern rubber thousands of years before anyone else.

Maya culture emphasizes natural cycles. One example is the seasonal harvest of crops.

Approximately 98 percent of residents in the town of Chichicastenango, Guatemala, are Maya K'iche'.

Religious beliefs are another example. One belief is that people move on to another life after death. In addition, the Maya value the ceiba tree. This tree connects the earth to the sky and afterlife.

Today, more than seven million Maya live around the world. Many still live in their native lands of Central America. They carry on their ancestors' traditions, such as religious rituals. Modern Maya speak more than 30 languages.

CHAPTER 3

GEOGRAPHY AND CLIMATE

Central America is an isthmus. An isthmus is a narrow piece of land with water on each side. This isthmus stretches approximately 1,140 miles (1,835 km). The Pacific Ocean lies to the west. The Caribbean Sea is to the east. These bodies of water connect through the Panama Canal. Gulfs line the coasts of Honduras, Panama, and Costa Rica. Central America also features many lakes and rivers. The largest lake is Lake Nicaragua.

Manuel Antonio National Park lies on the Pacific coast of Costa Rica.

A chain of mountains runs through western Central America. As a result, each country in the region has mountainous areas. The tallest peaks are in Guatemala.

Diverse geographies stretch across the region. For example, El Salvador is fairly small. But multiple landforms exist there. The country holds mountains and volcanoes. But there are also beaches and a tropical forest.

This variety brings many climates to Central America. Overall, the region tends to be tropical. That's because Central America lies near the equator. Tropical climates are warm. They feature wet seasons and dry seasons.

At the same time, climate depends on elevation and landforms. For this reason, the area's mountains and highlands have cool climates. And soil tends to be fertile. The elevation drops toward

▲ An active volcano can be found on the island of Ometepe in Nicaragua.

Central America's Caribbean coast. In Belize, swamps and lowlands are common. Those areas experience more humid climates.

However, **climate change** is affecting all of Central America. Extreme droughts have hit much of the Pacific coast. Sea-level rise is also occurring. Coasts are sinking. Because of this crisis, Central America's geography and climate are changing at an increasing pace.

CHAPTER 4

PLANTS AND ANIMALS

Central America takes up less than 1 percent of the land on Earth. Even so, the region holds a huge amount of biodiversity. Biodiversity is the variety of plants and animals that live in an area. Costa Rica alone supports 6 percent of the world's biodiversity. More than 13,000 different plants and animals live there.

Honduras is home to 700 species of birds. One of these birds is known as the Honduran Emerald.

The strawberry poison dart frog can only be found in Costa Rica, Panama, and Nicaragua.

▲ In 2019, fewer than 3,000 Honduran Emeralds were thought to be alive.

This hummingbird's throat glitters blue-green. The bird is found only in dry areas of Honduras.

In Panama and Costa Rica, amphibians and reptiles are common. In 2012, scientists identified a new frog species in Panama. The frog dyes peoples' hands yellow when they touch it.

Guatemala's diverse landforms support a wide variety of life. The country features 14 different **ecosystems**, including mountains, rivers, and coasts. Leatherback sea turtles often nest along the country's coasts. Leatherbacks are the largest turtles on Earth.

Central America's different climates also support a variety of plants. Some wildlife can only live in higher elevations. Other wildlife depends on tropical rainforests. For example, many tropical trees have thin bark. They get water easily from the humid air. Trees in other climates have thicker bark. That bark traps and stores water for dry seasons. Tropical plants are known for growing bright flowers. Bright colors are easier for animals and insects to find.

However, the region's biodiversity is in danger. One threat is deforestation. This process involves clearing forests for human development. People use this land for ranches, farms, and mining. But clearing forests forces wildlife to move.

In addition, climate change threatens wildlife across Central America. This crisis is causing storms to be stronger and more common. Scientists believe these storms may be one reason why biodiversity will drop.

Without certain species, ecosystems can become off-balance and struggle to survive. That's because each species plays a key role in the ecosystem where it lives. For instance, bats in Panama are important for controlling insect populations. The bats also help plants thrive. They spread seeds and pollinate flowers as they fly from place to place.

➤ THINK ABOUT IT

Do you think people are responsible for protecting the environment around them? If yes, what actions should they take? If no, why not?

▲ Belize's coral reefs are home to several kinds of ray, including southern stingrays.

In Belize, coral reefs on the coast provide homes to more than 500 species of fish. Humans and animals rely on these fish for food. For reasons such as these, many people are working on protecting Central America's plants and animals.

BIRDS OF CENTRAL AMERICA

Central America lies between two continents with very different climates. Parts of North America experience cold winters. But much of Central and South America is warm all year round.

For this reason, hundreds of bird species from North and South America migrate each year. In 2014, for example, more than 3.2 million birds flew over Panama City. They were migrating from Canada and the United States. Some birds stop in Central America to rest. Others stay there for part of the year. The region's many insects provide food for visiting birds. A variety of plants provide shelter.

The broad-winged hawk spends winters in Central and South America. It uses strong winds to soar and travel far distances. Western tanagers

▲ Motmots are birds that live in Central America. Their name is based on the sound they make.

are another migrating bird. These songbirds breed in dry forests of the western United States from April to August. Then they migrate south. They fly as far as Costa Rica. Some forests in Costa Rica are similar to the birds' US habitat.

Other birds in Central America do not migrate. They live in the region all year round. For instance, scarlet macaws live in several Central American countries. These birds are known for their blue, yellow, and red feathers. They squawk loudly and can be heard several miles away.

CHAPTER 5

NATURAL RESOURCES AND ECONOMY

Central America has a variety of resources, including minerals and gold. Copper is mined in Panama. Oil is drilled in Guatemala. Crops also fuel many economies. Corn and beans grow well in El Salvador. Its climate is cool and dry. Belize is warm and humid. Fruits such as bananas grow there. Coffee beans are another major crop. In 2019, the region made 10 percent of the world's arabica. This type of coffee bean is very popular.

A farmer in eastern El Salvador waters his crops.

At the same time, not all farming happens on a large scale. Many Indigenous people farm only for themselves and their communities. These small economies often conflict with larger industries. For instance, Costa Rica's and Belize's economies depend on tourism. For this reason, Costa Rica and Belize protect certain natural areas. In those areas, they ban activities such as logging or fishing. However, these areas are often home to Indigenous groups. Many groups have depended on the areas for thousands of years. Those groups face conflict when they try to farm or fish.

In the region's cities, many people work in factories. Some countries, such as the United States, prefer to buy goods from Central America. US companies can pay Central American workers less than US workers. Central American **textile** companies also compete with Asian companies.

◢ Approximately 5 percent of all ocean trade goes through the Panama Canal.

The region's companies make many products. But the countries are small. Their businesses cannot produce everything people need. For this reason, Central America **imports** goods from around the world. Some major products include construction materials and machinery.

Countries make the money to pay for these products in different ways. Panama receives a large amount of money from the Panama Canal.

That's because ships have to pay Panama to use the canal. Other countries sell food and goods around the world. The United States is a major trading partner. So are countries in western Europe.

This kind of trade plays a huge role in the region. In fact, five Central American countries signed a trade agreement with the United States in 2004. The deal was known as the Central America Free Trade Agreement (CAFTA). CAFTA gave the United States cheaper access to goods. In exchange, Central American countries hoped for economic growth.

➤ **THINK ABOUT IT**

What might be the advantages of importing goods?
What might be the disadvantages?

CAFTA did bring more jobs and money to the region. However, some US companies took advantage of the agreement. They paid workers very low wages. They did not share wealth equally. These problems continue to challenge the people and governments of Central America.

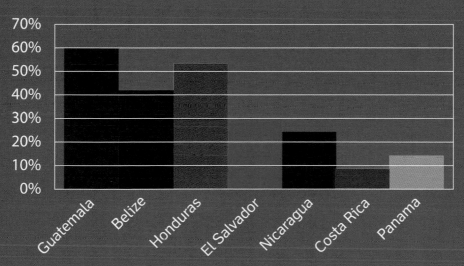

POVERTY RATES IN CENTRAL AMERICA, 2017 ◁

This graph shows the percentage of people living on less than $5.50 a day, defined here as poverty.

CHAPTER 6

GOVERNMENT AND POLITICS

All countries in Central America have democratic governments. In this system, citizens vote for their leaders. People elect a president in each country except Belize. As a former British colony, Belize is part of the British Commonwealth. Queen Elizabeth II is Belize's head of state. And a prime minister leads the country. The voting age is 18 in all countries except Nicaragua. It is 16 there.

Queen Elizabeth II (left) meets with Dean Barrow, the prime minister of Belize, at Buckingham Palace in London, England.

Many Indigenous peoples continue to struggle against their governments. For instance, Guatemalan and Belizean governments allow companies to use Maya land. Maya communities try to protect their lands. But activists are often arrested or killed for their efforts.

The Naso people in Panama have also been trying to protect their land. In 2018, Panama's government passed a law giving the Naso rights to their land. But the president blocked the law. The decision went to Panama's Supreme Court. The Naso hoped the court would side with them.

Corruption has been a problem in some Central American governments. Since 2009, for example, many people in Honduras have protested their leaders. That year, a US-backed **coup** replaced Honduras's president. The new government funded corrupt groups. Much of that

▲ Honduran farmers carry a picture of Indigenous activist Berta Cáceres to protest her assassination in 2016.

money ended up back in lawmakers' pockets. President Juan Orlando Hernández was likely involved in some of these problems. In 2017, Hernández won reelection. But many people believed he had manipulated the election.

In 2018, Nicaraguan citizens started protesting as well. President Daniel Ortega had been elected in 2006. But he had made the government less democratic. He had taken control of all parts of government, such as the Supreme Court.

Ortega tried to control the 2018 protests using force. Police and soldiers killed hundreds of people. Many citizens kept protesting. But tens of thousands of people fled to Costa Rica. They hid from Ortega's forces. They faced harsh charges if they returned. Some may have even faced torture.

The region's governments also have conflicts with one another. For example, Belize and Guatemala have long disagreed about their shared border. Two-thirds of the land Belize controls is in question. Guatemala has claimed this territory as its own. The International Court of Justice agreed to settle the issue.

> # THINK ABOUT IT

What makes a government democratic? What can cause that government to be more or less democratic?

Nicaraguan people march in protest of President Daniel Ortega in 2018.

In addition, certain governments have struggled to address crises in their own countries. In 2019, many people in El Salvador, Guatemala, and Honduras were living in poverty. These governments did not have enough money to spend on public needs. Crime and gang violence were also common in these three countries. For these reasons, hundreds of thousands of people left their homes. Some traveled north to Mexico or the United States, looking for a better life.

CHAPTER 7

PEOPLE AND CULTURE

The population of Central America is approximately 50 million. Guatemala's population is the largest by far. More than 16 million people live there. Most other countries are home to between three million and nine million people.

Approximately 40 percent of Central Americans live in rural areas. The region's economies remain largely based on farming. But cities are growing.

Bríbri are one of the largest Indigenous groups in Costa Rica.

Most people in Central America have mixed ancestry. Many have European, African, and American Indian roots. These people are sometimes known as mestizos.

In every country, **colonialism** changed people's way of life and even their language use. Its effects can still be seen today. For example, Spanish is the official language of six countries. And English is the official language of Belize. Even so, many people in Belize also speak Kriol. This language is based on English. But American Indian and African languages are blended with it.

Christianity is the region's main religion. Eighty percent of people are Catholic. But many traditions blend religious, Indigenous, and Spanish roots. Indigenous peoples also continue traditional practices. People have celebrations for the dead, the saints, and the harvest.

▲ Many Indigenous Emberá people live along the Chagres River in Panama.

More than 25 Indigenous groups live in Central America. The Kakawira and Lenca live in El Salvador. The Emberá live in Panama. Approximately 50 percent of the Maya population lives in Guatemala. The K'iche' are the largest group of Maya in Guatemala. Maya peoples also live in Belize, including the Mopan.

The Indigenous Miskito people live in Honduras and Nicaragua. These people also have African ancestry. They fish and farm along the Caribbean coast. Cassava is one of their main crops.

In Belize, Garifuna culture is especially strong. Garifuna music often features drumming with Afro-Indigenous roots. And Garifuna music today often blends many genres, including reggae, salsa, and hip-hop.

Other people in Central America have Afro-Caribbean ancestry as well. Panama and Belize have the largest Black populations in the region. However, Black and Indigenous peoples have faced many difficulties in Central America. The region's main cultures often favor white and mestizo people. Racism against other peoples is common. Even so, Black and Indigenous peoples have been working for their rights.

▲ The United Nations has declared that Garifuna language, music, and dance are masterful cultural traditions.

Life in Central America is a combination of cultures. Meals often combine Spanish, Indigenous, and African ideas. Meals are based on fresh foods from different regions. Corn, beans, rice, pineapple, and seafood are common. In El Salvador, people have corn festivals. In Belize, people hold a chocolate festival in a mainly Maya area. From land to sea and farms to cities, the cultures of Central America are incredibly diverse.

FOCUS ON
CENTRAL AMERICA

Write your answers on a separate piece of paper.

1. Write a paragraph describing the main ideas of Chapter 7.

2. The United States has influenced many events in Central America's history. What role do you think outside countries should play in Central America?

3. What country first invaded Central America?

    A. the United States

    B. Mexico

    C. Spain

4. Why might Indigenous peoples have conflicts with Central American governments?

    A. The governments are trying to make Indigenous languages illegal.

    B. Modern-day countries are formed on lands taken from Indigenous peoples.

    C. Indigenous peoples are trying to take over the governments.

Answer key on page 48.

GLOSSARY

civilization
A large group of people with a shared history and culture.

climate change
A human-caused global crisis involving long-term changes in Earth's temperature and weather patterns.

colonialism
A system where one country controls another group of people in a different area and uses those people for the country's benefit.

conquistadores
Leaders of the Spanish invasion of the Americas.

corruption
Dishonest or illegal acts, especially by powerful people.

coup
An overthrow of a government by a small number of people, often involving violence.

ecosystems
Communities of living things and how they interact with their surrounding environments.

imports
Buys and brings products in from another country.

Indigenous
Native to a region, or belonging to ancestors who lived in a region before colonists arrived.

textile
Relating to fabric or weaving.

TO LEARN MORE

BOOKS

Kott, Jennifer, Kristi Streiffert, and Debbie Nevins. *Nicaragua*. New York: Cavendish Square, 2016.

LaPierre, Yvette. *Engineering the Panama Canal*. Minneapolis: Abdo Publishing, 2018.

Spilsbury, Louise. *The Mayans*. Chicago: Capstone, 2017.

NOTE TO EDUCATORS

Visit **www.focusreaders.com** to find lesson plans, activities, links, and other resources related to this title.

INDEX

Belize, 5, 7, 10, 12, 19, 25, 29–30, 33, 35–36, 38, 42–45

Central America Free Trade Agreement (CAFTA), 32–33

Costa Rica, 6–7, 13, 17, 21–22, 27, 30, 33, 38

El Salvador, 6–7, 10, 13, 18, 29, 33, 39, 43, 45

Garifuna, 44

Guatemala, 5–7, 9–10, 12–13, 18, 22, 29, 33, 36, 38–39, 41, 43

Hernández, Juan Orlando, 37

Honduras, 6–7, 12, 17, 21–22, 33, 36, 39, 44

Itzá, 12

K'iche', 10, 43

Kriol, 42

Maya, 10, 14–15, 36, 43, 45

Miskito, 12, 44

Mopan, 10, 43

Nicaragua, 6–7, 10, 12–13, 33, 35, 37, 44

Ortega, Daniel, 37–38

Panama, 6–7, 12–13, 17, 22, 24, 29, 31–33, 36, 43–44

Panama Canal, 6, 12, 17, 31–32

Pipil, 10

Answer Key: 1. Answers will vary; 2. Answers will vary; 3. C; 4. B